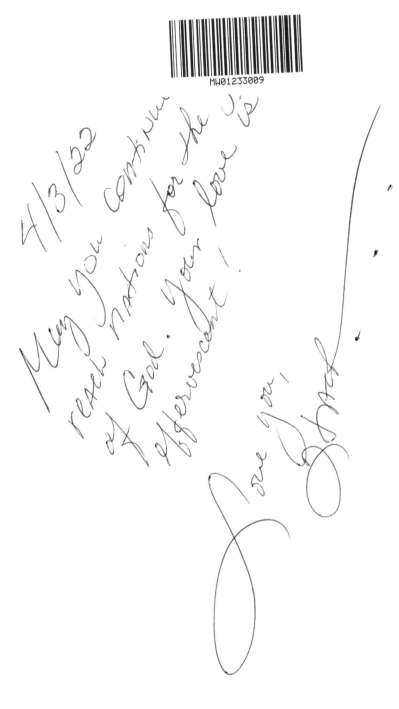

4/3/22

May you continue to reach nations for the 🙂 of God. Your love is effervescent!

Love you,
[signature]

THE MOST IMPORTANT WORD

HEWLETTE PEARSON

CREATION
HOUSE

THE MOST IMPORTANT WORD by Hewlette A. C. Pearson
Published by Creation House Books
A Charisma Media Company
600 Rinehart Road
Lake Mary, Florida 32746
www.charismamedia.com

Most of the individuals herein are composite characters whose names have been changed to preserve their anonymity. Any resemblance to actual persons living or dead is purely coincidental.

Unless otherwise noted, all Scripture quotations are from *The Message: The Bible in Contemporary English*, copyright © 1993, 1994, 1995, 1996, 2000, 2001, 2002. Used by permission of NavPress Publishing Group.

Scripture quotations marked KJV are from the King James Version of the Bible.

Scripture quotations marked NIV are from the Holy Bible, New International Version. Copyright © 1973, 1978, 1984, International Bible Society. Used by permission.

All translations of "I Love You" throughout the text and end materials are taken from "I Love You! In 122 Languages" provided courtesy of Roger Darlington. The complete list can be accessed online at http://www.rogerdarlington.me.uk/Iloveyou.html.

Design Director: Bill Johnson
Cover design by Terry Clifton

Copyright © 2011 by Hewlette A. C. Pearson
All rights reserved

Visit the author's website: www.hewlettepearson.com

Library of Congress Cataloging-in-Publication Data: 2011928568
International Standard Book Number: 978-1-61638-594-1

First edition

11 12 13 14 15 — 9 8 7 6 5 4 3 2 1
Printed in Canada

In loving memory of Brenda Waters, an indefatigable musician, song writer, choir director, comedienne, to name a few, and a wonderful friend who taught me how to appreciate the beauty and love that I bring to others.

To Christopher Clark who left us suddenly…I miss your hugs and hearing you call my mom, "Goddy."

Acknowledgments

$\mathcal{T}$HANK YOU SO much, Felix and Gretel Pearson (Mom and Dad) for being my greatest supporters, and Dr. Caretha F. Crawford (my mentor). You all have taught me well…I am still learning and growing. I forge ahead with your continued support.

Julianne Pearson, Minnie Turner, Ruth "Blessen" Franks, and Lea J. Philippe, thank you for believing in me and cheering me on along the way. Your encouragement at different intervals in this journey pushed me to take this all the way to publication.

Kathy Hazzard and Verdine Parker, thank you for introducing me to the living legend of contemporary Gospel music, Andraé Crouch. You trusted that he would believe in the content of the book and be willing to contribute his voice to it. I am grateful to you.

Andraé Crouch, I am just speechless when it comes to the impact you have had on my life over the past two decades. Your music has inspired and pushed me to live life out loud! I have been strengthened and encouraged to also continue in my walk with God. I'm looking forward to more music from that inexhaustible well God placed on the inside of you. Thank you for agreeing to lend your voice to this *Most Important Word*.

Without the response of every person I interviewed and included in this book, there would be very little to share. Thank you for those "special moments" when you cried, laughed, sighed, or just sat silent for a moment pondering. The rest of the world will now benefit and hopefully experience the many emotions I felt while conversing with you.

To every incarcerated and ex-offender student who sat under my teaching, thank you. Spending time with you in our training classes helped me to realize that love is real! Your love of freedom and tenacity toward life inspire me.

Contents

Foreword

*T*HERE IS A powerful saying in the Bible, "For God so loved the world, that he gave his only begotten Son, that whosoever believeth in him should not perish, but have everlasting life" (John 3:16, KJV). In Hewlette Pearson's book, *The Most Important Word*, she deals with the word *love*. She has interviewed many people about what their definition of love is. She asks, "What is your feeling when love is expressed to you? How do you show love?" Hewlette has shown that regardless of color, age, custom, and occupation, people's lives are affected similarly.

Her book will guide you back to the love of God, the most important love there is. It will help you to focus on Jesus' love for humankind. Jesus loved us so much; He was willing to die on the cross. "Greater love hath no man than this, that a man lay down his life for his friends" (John 15:13, KJV). This indeed is the greatest act of love.

Many years ago as I was thinking about God's love for me, I decided to write a song called "My Tribute." In that song I asked . . .

> How can I say thanks for the things You have done for me?
> Things so undeserved yet You gave to prove Your love for
>   me.
> The voices of a million angels could not express my
>   gratitude.
> All that I am, and ever hope to be, I owe it all to Thee.[1]

God's love raised Jesus from the dead for our salvation. And so, no matter what you or I do, His love is always there to forgive us, to save us, and to help us show our gratitude.

This message from Hewlette Pearson will continue to remind us, as we journey through life, to never forget to love and help others.

—ANDRAÉ CROUCH, LEGENDARY CONTEMPORARY GOSPEL ARTIST
PASTOR, NEW CHRIST MEMORIAL CHURCH OF GOD IN CHRIST
SAN FERNANDO, CALIFORNIA

Introduction

*U*NCUT . . . uncensored . . . real.

That is what life is anyway . . . correct?

Well, the idea for this book came about when I began to realize something—how often people mentioned the word *recession*. From late 2008 to mid-year 2009, I felt so overwhelmed by the plethora of news stories, both in print and electronic media, about the recession. It seemed as if it opened and closed every newscast. Although I did not subscribe to it as I made sure to focus on more positive things, I wondered in what way, if any, it was affecting people. Were people being perplexed, frustrated, and anxious just about their jobs and finances, or were they also concerned about people around them?

Often when we are faced with lack, we find ourselves doing, for the most part, one of two things—giving or hoarding. In other words, we either look to share with others, pulling our resources together, or we shift to secretly storing away things for ourselves, as if for self-preservation nonetheless.

Did or has the recession also affected how we respond to or treat one another? Have we become recessed in our love for each other as a result of tough economic times?

Well, to answer these questions, I set off on a journey to query the minds of random individuals whom I ran into on the street, sat beside on the subway, connected with on a social site, waited with in the doctor's office, walked alongside at a Race for the Cure walkathon, and met through mutual friends in various cities of the United States. As I thought to just stop at about twenty or twenty-five interviews, I found myself, without thought or preparation, continuing to walk up to people to ask the questions. As I continued to be captivated by the emotional impact the questions had on some, I pressed forward. It was as if the questions ignited a fire that was soon to go out . . . like hope was reborn.

As I was impacted by strangers in such a profound way, I thought,

1

"I wonder how a few of my family and friends would respond to the questions." I took a few days to do visits and make phone calls to interrupt their "busy" lives just to answer my questions.

Wow! I could hardly hold myself together as there was so much energy being exchanged as they shared. I found myself crying, laughing, and hoping with them as well. The time came, though, that I had to "put the brakes on." Folks started hearing about my "little" project and began approaching me to give their input.

The participants—from varied age groups, occupations, cultural, socioeconomic, ethnic, and religious backgrounds—shared their responses to the three questions I posed:

1. What is your definition of love?

2. How do you show love?

3. How do you feel when love is shown or expressed to you?

My initial approach brought varied responses. Some found the questions hard to answer; others paused for a while before answering; some asked if they could think about it and get back with me; and others seemed as if they had been holding the answer for quite some time and were grateful for the opportunity to release it.

Laughter...

Regret...

Tears...

Pain...

Hope...

Forgiveness...

These emotions overwhelmed some as they shared their responses with me.

Although their answers are real and moving, several of the respondents requested that I not use their real names in order to protect their identity. Giving in to this request was small compared to the honor of sharing their story with you. It is my hope that as you read their "heart," you will somehow experience something that we all need—love.

Oh, by the way…I did some cursory research to obtain, in as many languages present in the earth, the phrase "I love you" to remind us to use it as much as we can. As you well know…love is truly universal.

Uncut…uncensored…real…

Read on…

The Most Important Word.

Chapter 1

The Kindergartner

What is your definition of love?

Hmm...I don't really know.

How do you know mommy and daddy love you?

Because they tell me and show me. They take me places like movies and McDonald's to get something to eat. They treat you nicely and stuff...and bring stuff so you can have fun. They check on you every night...that you are asleep and stuff. They help you through stuff and help you ride your bike and stuff and practice doing things. They help you play your piano and drums. They read a book to you at nighttime and kiss you at night and tuck you in. They put a teddy bear beside you so you can go to sleep...and stuff.

How do you show love to mommy and daddy?

By being good and stuff...and by saying yes when they talk to me. When they ask me something, I answer it and stuff...and do whatever they say.

How do you feel when someone shows you love?

I feel happy and kind.

—Tré

Chapter 2

Female Ex-Gangbanger

*W*ELL, I'M FORTY-TWO years old, and I've had plenty of bumps in the road...more like hills if you ask me [laughing]. I just come home; I've been locked up half of my life...more than half...and I'm now in transition, getting my life together. You're asking me to define love...hmmm. To me, love is giving unconditionally; it's with no strings attached. It's unconditional...yes, unconditional.

I show love by giving whatever I can. Like I said, it's unconditional, you know, whether it be in a relationship or just being with anybody I encounter. I'm one of those people that even if it's people I just meet, when it's all said and done, I tell 'em, "I love you." So I understand. If I could give you an example of how I show love, it would be this: I like to help the senior citizens and the mentally challenged, the homeless, the addicts that are just really far gone. I like to help those that are the underdogs, so to speak, people that other people overlook or take for granted.

I went and cut a friend's hair; he lives in a transition home for elders and the mentally unstable. And when I cut his hair, there was an older man who came downstairs and asked me, "You cut hair? Can you cut my hair?" I said, "Sure." "But how much you charge?" I told him to just give me five dollars. He started asking everybody for money to make up to five dollars. After I saw all he was going through just to get five dollars, I just told him not to worry about it; I'd do it at no charge.

I cut his hair and he was so happy...he kept saying how good his haircut looked. His gratitude to me was...wow! It felt better than getting high...that ultimate high 'cause it felt so good that he really, really appreciated it. I know he did, because I could tell from just looking at him that he was deprived of a lot of things...now, where he is. I don't know of his past, but where he is now...I can tell.

I cut a lady's hair too who was there. She was just so happy, and I felt so light...like I wasn't even touching the ground. I can't...I can't describe it. By the way, I left my number, so I know they'll be calling back [laughing]. I just really feel good about that.

When I experience love...man, I can't really say the words. I can't find the words to say when I experience love. Love is priceless to me...the feeling is priceless. It makes me feel encouraged; it lifts me; I feel that I can accomplish things that I could not do before.

—"Ms. Second Chance"

"I Love You"

Afrikaans	Ek is lief vir jou
Albanian	Te dua
Arabic	Ah'bika [to a man]
	Ah'bik [to a woman]
Armenian	Yes qez sirum em
Assyrian	Kedamtookh brikhta
Azerbaijani	Men seni sevirem
Bamougoum	Guo me ye te
Bangladeshi	Ami tomake valobashi
Basque	Maite zaitut
Belarusian	Ya tabe kahayu
Bemba	Nalikutemwa
Bengali	Aami tomaake bhaalo baashi
Bosnian	Volim te
Bulgarian	Obicham te
Burmese	Chit pa de

Chapter 3

The Mortician

*L*OVE IS AN ingredient. I believe that is what the world needs today. That ingredient may not have a substance; it's just an ingredient. It could be a spirit; it could be a feeling…it's nothing you can hold.

I show love through my work and mostly through my art that we practice here at the funeral home. I do have family time, but most of my time is spent at work, so I do a lot of love through my job. I show love through my work by trying to make most of my families do the "closing" when they lose a loved one, and I try to bond that gap between life and death. I am a great embalmer, so I show love to the families by the way I handle the body of their loved one.

I feel happy when love is expressed or shown to me, most of all. Again, it's that substance, that ingredient that's needed with life.

—"THE CLOSER"

Chapter 4

The Police Officer

*F*IRST OF ALL, not to sound cliché-ish, I think that God is love, and I think that everything that embodies God is love—from discipline, to blessings, to trials, to joys.

In this profession, when I joined the police department, I initially joined because I had a desire to be an outreach ministry for the police department...being a police officer that a child could come up to if they were lost, or a caring individual that could step into the middle for a domestic violence situation and hear both sides and be fair...and at the same time try and resolve it to the point where the couple could seek counseling as opposed to separating. To me, to the department...it's a needed thing in being a police officer, because you deal with a lot of people who feel that they are destitute...you know, degenerates, people who have had experiences in their life that have caused them to not know love. So being a first responder...you may be the only love that they know or the first bit of compassion that they see that leads to love. So it is important to me, as a police officer, to polish that character...that trait...so that you can provide that in your care—in your handling of prisoners as well as victims.

Well...I would say I feel no different than the victims, the prisoners, and the people that I spoke of before when others show me love. When you receive love or you're touched by love, it changes you in so many ways. It can be the difference between a good day and a bad day...loving words, a loving touch. I think that it's a nice feeling, you know, when people embrace you and say that they love you...whether it be verbally or physically—again, like I said, with a touch or smile. Being in the profession that we're in, a lot of times police are portrayed in the media in a certain way, so it's a nice thing when a citizen walks up to you and says thank you for the profession that you chose that keeps us safe. To me that's an expression of love. I don't think you have to know somebody twenty years to love them; the appreciation that's shown in the service that you provide is a form of love to me, whether it be from your family members or citizens. It's a good feeling.

I think that the world lacks a lot of love, and I think that the times we are living in—the recession, the hopelessness that's felt throughout the land—keeping in mind the times that we are living in, you have to go the extra mile and be an example. You have to lead by example when it comes to love. I'm a Christian, and my life might be the only Bible some people ever read. I understand that when you make mistakes, you should be the first person to say "I'm sorry," or "I apologize," and try everything you can to correct the situation or bridge a gap that will lead to correction. Unfortunately, sometimes forgiveness, which is an act of love (because love is a verb that requires an action), does not mean reconciling, but you can still pray for the individual and do it in love.

What the world is in need of now, more than ever before, is love, sweet love. But the most important love that people need is God's love. I think that's what makes it sweet!

—"THE PROTECTOR"

Chapter 5

Homeless Vietnam Veteran

$\mathcal{M}$ Y DEFINITION OF love…well, it is a pretty dynamic question because I think there are a lot of categories of love. Like in the Bible, it talks about agape love, and there are eros and filial love. So I think if we're going to make a general statement about love, the most appropriate definition would be "agape" when talking about loving one another, life around us…the air we breathe…the caring we give. I think love is really in that respect…it can be defined simply as having a sense or emotion to care about the environment around you, that it stays healthy and you feel good about helping to accomplish that. And I think that is the simplest way to explain love.

I think there is a lot deeper you can go in this thing, like a pet for instance. You can come and pet your dog…come home and have a superficial feeling for your dog 'cause there is companionship there. Or you can really go out and do things with the dog and gain a real personal deeper sense and feeling about the pet, or a person…and so I think it has a greater feedback that we really don't think about. Love…eros—that deeper love—is really important as well. It really helps to drive our society and replenish our species, which is very important. I mean…all of the other love would not matter if we didn't have replenishment. I think a mixture of both…if we can have a real deep agape relationship…I think that really feeds in to having a deeper eros feeling of love.

It's really simplistic answers, I think, yet so multidimensional. It's like artwork…"Beauty is in the eye of the beholder." And so I think if you would ask another person, they would have different feelings about what love means to them…and I think it is probably correct for them and mine is correct for me.

Love is really an elusive butterfly to try to define.

My answer to how I show love may seem complex. I think the more vulnerable a person becomes, the deeper the feeling. It's hard to explain because I am psychologically projecting, you know, my definition and my feelings about things compared to someone else's...but anyway, the more vulnerable you become, the more you have a need to be helped by the fabric around you...I mean, it's like the trees for instance. When it's a hot sunny day, ninety degrees for instance, unconsciously you are not considering that you really have a feeling about that tree because it's bringing shade; it's helping you...it's a cooperation between you and that plant...and I think on a ninety-degree day we become vulnerable if we don't have air conditioning that we can walk into. So it's a vulnerability, and so we find a shady tree and sit down underneath it and unconsciously we have a cooperation going. And it is a love... "Thank you very much...I'm vulnerable and you've fulfilled my need." And so I think the same thing can be said for people or pets. For example, maybe I'm feeling a little lonely...my pet fills in those lonely gaps between my friendships that I have.

Relating it to my homelessness...that's a really vulnerable scenario, especially in this day and age. It's such a jet-set kind of attitude between people, and they kind of miss those needs...you know...like you can walk up to a shady tree and sit down, and you don't have to ask the tree, "May I sit here and enjoy your shade?" And so there has to be a mutual relationship. But I think that it is very important that the more vulnerable people become, the more we should try to become receptive in trying to help someone. We need to understand that we need to help other people. We don't need to have to expect anything in return except for a feeling that we've helped build ourselves up by helping build up the fabric around us. That's what it really does. It doesn't seem like that, but in the long run, if we strengthen the society around us, even if it's only psychologically, we strengthen ourselves in return.

I think it is important, whether homeless or not, that we go and search out each other's needs. If we become receptive to what our needs really are, we will find that the people who are rich have greater needs than the people who are poor because all forms of refuge has its price. Sometimes being rich and powerful...you become a captive...you become secluded and can't just go and walk out in the open...so you become a prisoner to a need—"I'm lonely and can't socialize with anybody I want to because I'm famous or rich and powerful..."

So sometimes we cannot say that the needs are only at the bottom because the greatest needs can be at the top end and we miss it because we have this preconceived notion that they have everything, but don't realize that the more a person has, the more they become a prisoner to it. I've felt that way myself…

How does it make me feel when others show me love? Well, I'll have to say that it is better to give than to receive…so I think to receive love is fantastic. But if I had my way about it, I think…if I had one choice or another, I'd rather show love than to receive it. But I think you really have to receive love…genuine love. I love receiving love, but I love giving love…in my definition of love and always trying to maintain a true movement toward the modification of understanding what love is, not only for myself and my definition, but also how people are receptive or not receptive of my giving of love. There are so many ways for these things to be misinterpreted, so I think what we really need to do is move some of these stumbling blocks of interpretation out of the way first, so we can see clearly and learn what each person's need and definition of love is.

—Daniel

Chapter 6

Tow Truck Driver

*L*OVE IS—TO ME—KNOWING that someone cares about you deeply and can go that extra mile for you no matter what, and is always there for you.

As a female tow truck driver for AAA, I show love the same way I get love; you show it back…you always give back…you give to others what you want to get back. Being a female tow truck driver, I show love by smiling and treating people with respect. I get a lot of people who are shocked to see me. All I can do is do my job and smile and pay it no attention. Sometimes people say very nasty things to me…I get comments from ladies, but the majority of the time they're from men. For example, they'll say, "Well I guess it's equal opportunity…" Some will even mention that the women are doing what the men are doing now, but hey…a job is a job; anybody can do it.

I've had people "cuss" me out…using profanity, but sometimes I get interesting responses. One time I got a call to fix a flat…three guys riding in a van couldn't locate the spare or change the tire. When I showed up and got out of my truck, you could see that they were surprised I was a female and wondered whether or not I could do the job. It was pretty awkward for them 'cause people were passing by and I, being a female, was down there on the ground changing a tire while three men stood and watched me. I got the job done, though.

I feel happy…I feel very happy when I'm shown love. I feel very appreciated… appreciated. That just means someone else out there loves you more than you love yourself.

—B. LOVETTE

"I Love You"

Cambodian	Soro lahn nhee ah
Cantonese	Ngo oi ney
Catalan	T'estimo
Cheyenne	Ne mohotatse
Chinese	Wo ie ni
Cornish	My a'th kar
Corsican	Ti tengu caru [to a man]
	Ti tengu cara [to a woman]
Creole	Mwen renmen w
Croatian	Ja te volim
Czech	Miluji tě

Chapter 7

Athlete and Cancer Survivor

*L*OVE ACCEPTS YOU regardless of your flaws; it looks beyond and through. Love is unselfish, thoughtful, and forgiving of the most painful violations. Love is flexible yet stern and consistent.

Love hurts too. Love is honest, with a touch of honey (to soften the inevitable blow). Love is…"Now baby, this is going to hurt mama [belt in hand] more than it hurts you." Love is…"I got to tell you the truth because I love you." I've learned from my parents and the Bible that chastisement comes from a place of love. Proverbs 3:11–12 states, "My son, do not despise the LORD's discipline and do not resent his rebuke, because the LORD disciplines those he loves, as a father [parent] the son [child] he delights in" (NIV).

It's kind of hard to nail down an exact definition of love. *Love is doing unto others, as you would have them do unto you.*

I show love by:

- Giving of my time, talents and money to my family, friends, community, students, and church family

- Disciplining and accepting discipline (adults can be corrected and show vulnerability)

- Working to provide for my daughter and my foster child

- Forgiving as Christ has instructed me to do…even in the hardest scenarios

- Speaking a kind word

- Giving hugs and kisses

- Being silly or funny to cheer up a person

- Being consistent

- Making tough decisions for the good of the family

- Spending quality time with others

- Making surprise telephone calls or visits

- Giving expected (birthdays, anniversaries, etc.) and "unexpected" gifts

- Taking care of and building my physical and spiritual body; I cannot love if I'm physically unable to move, and I cannot love if my spirit is weak.

When others show me love, I feel worthy, priceless, beautiful, sexy, intelligent, useful, vital, necessary, needed, a sense of belonging, special, empowered, supported, happy, appreciated, and accepted.

—E. FRENCH

Chapter 8

Classical and Jazz Musician

*M*Y DEFINITION OF love is just the bottom line of treating others as you want to be treated...you know what I'm saying? I think it starts with yourself 'cause once you love yourself, you'll be able to love someone else. But basically for me...it's treating somebody with respect...respect my space, I respect your space...respect the fact that you have a voice to bring, otherwise you would not be here.

I'm a giver...and I have to balance that too 'cause sometimes I give to my detriment... and people take your kindness for weakness, but I'm a giver...that's what I do. I'm a nurturer, a giver...I always have people around me—which I love...I love it—but that's the way I support those whom I have means to support and they're in a situation. I work a lot with the homeless community downtown. I volunteer...that's my job...really. I love it...I really do. I try to give back...my mom's favorite thing is "to those who've been given much, to those much is required," and so I take that seriously.

I feel good when love is expressed to me. I don't know what good is, but my good is good. You see, I'm really deep into that 'cause I'm a musician and I'm around people whom I have these deep spiritual discussions with all the time. Good for me is knowing that I'm in my right personal space and I've treated you accordingly. It's like in my house...it's a big community thing...everybody shares and shares alike, but it's also the respect of saying if that's the last slice of pizza and it's not yours, don't take it.

To me it is the giving and receiving in kind...it takes me back to the "do unto others..." thing. I try to know that this kind of path that I'm walking is right for me, and in that I respect everybody else's right. And to me that is a form of love that says, "I respect you. I love you for the fact that you have something that is yours." That's it... in a nutshell.

—D. E. "TREBLE CLEF"

"I Love You"

Danish	Jeg elsker dig
Dutch	Ik hou van jou
Ecuador	Quechua canda munani
English	I love you
Esperanto	Mi amas vin
Estonian	Ma armastan sind
Ethiopian	Afgreki'

Chapter 9

Attempted Rape Victim

Tó tell you the truth, I don't even know if I really know the definition of love aside from being a parent to my children and knowing I have to give them that motherly love. Could it be culture? Maybe, because in my culture we don't really show love with affection. We show it by providing food, shelter, clothes, and so on. Hearing my parents say, "I love you," was not something I experienced. It was not until I came to this country and noticed how other parents would love on their kids both in affection and in saying, "I love you," that I realized the importance of expressing it.

Love should be a door whereby you can come through to express what is going on with you. For me personally...when I was about twenty-two, I told my mom "I love you" when I was about to hang up the phone...but it was like pulling teeth to get a response from her. You could hear the stutter in her voice as she tried to respond. She eventually grew into being accustomed to it because I began to express love to her before we ended our conversation. Now my mom beats me to saying it before we end our conversation by phone.

I am still waiting to experience love, though.

Seeing tragedy and breaking down with sorrow for the individual...is that love? If so, then I believe that I know that aspect of love. Like Hurricane Katrina...I felt so sorry about what happened, and cried for days because I could not help like I really wanted to. Well, I guess talking to you about this type of love...I guess it is compassionate love.

What I have been through has probably affected how I look at love. The attempted rape that occurred to me was so hurtful on several fronts. I was scarred by the experience, both by the perpetrator (who was a church member) and by the church folks whom I worshiped with for more than fourteen years. The church, instead of protecting and showing love to me, were more concerned about their image. It was easier to portray me as a liar than rally around me. So right now...I don't really know how to answer the question. Maybe one day I will be able to answer the question.

I struggle with relationships now because I have such high expectations of people because of all that I have gone through. I guess I am looking for the opposite of what I went through. I look for loyalty, stability, and trust...yeah, those things.

My love comes in the form of compassion. I love helping people!

If I hear that you are hungry, I will use extreme measures to make sure you get something to eat, even if it means I go without so you can have something. I see purpose in people, and believe that my contribution will help to move them along in achieving it even if it is for them to live for the next day.

When others show me love, I feel complete...like mission accomplished! Because love is a two-way street, I feel that what I've shown is bouncing back to me. The circle is complete...it is balanced whether it is a mother to child, husband to wife, friend to friend...and so on.

—M. E. London

Chapter 10

US Contractor in Afghanistan

*H*MM... My definition of love? I would have to say it has to be surrounded with concern, compassion. The love has to be expressed in words and backed up with actions. I would define that as being compassionate, concerned, and an action showing expression toward somebody whom you really have strong feelings about.

I show love in few different aspects...like sending cards, phone calls to my wife or somebody whom I really love...my parents, family members...just being there to support them with a wide range of things. If they have goals, I'll be there to support them in meeting their goals; if they have some shortcomings, I'll support them and say, "Hey, you can do better."

In my experience, both as an ex-military person and as a contractor working in Afghanistan, I see love playing a part in what I do because of why we are really there in Afghanistan. We're not really there because of land, oil, or for some type of profit for the government. We are there because of what transpired in 2001...9/11. We're there to capture the individuals who were behind the whole event that took place in September 2001. So I'm there to support the military members there [on base] on a spiritual level as well as a mental level.

When I say "spiritual level," I'm talking about what I personally do outside of my job. Because they have a number of events...the gospel service that I'm a part of, etc., we get a lot of young people over there who have never really been in that type of environment, being put in harm's way...so-called "harm's way" because it's really not that much harm over there right now. But just to support them and let them know that spiritually, if you trust and believe in God, everything is going to work out fine. And if it doesn't, because of your relationship with God, you're going to a better place anyway. So we are there...there just to support them.

I feel grateful when love is shown to me. Sometimes I really can't explain it because when love is shown to you by somebody you don't expect to show their love, it just kind of gets you off guard and you're just dumbfounded…speechless. But when it's really shown to me, I'm appreciative. I'm not a man who really expresses a lot of emotions, but when you really do something that touches me…yeah…yeah.

I think that is something everybody should be able to experience. There's a lot of young people whom I run across every day over in Afghanistan who never had love expressed or expressed love to anybody or never felt love from anybody. So that's one of the reasons I feel that God has me over in Afghanistan, just to minister to a group of people who have never experienced love.

It's not a hard ground to tap into because when you really get these young people's attention and they feel your concern and you are sincere with them, they will open up and share some things with you that they haven't shared with anybody else. Then I can really express my love toward them letting them know, "Yes, because you are a child of God and I love you, I want the best for you…I don't even know who you are…I'm just meeting you over a few weeks, but because of the love that I have for Christ and the love Christ has given me to love other people, I love you." I just have to show that love to them and express it too.

When I express this to them, a lot of them are shocked…because somebody whom they barely know can say, "I love you." They really don't know how to take it, initially, without you spending additional time with them. But they begin to feel that love I expressed to them earlier, so they are really receptive to it after a while. These young people I speak of are all American soldiers 'cause they don't allow us to minister to the Afghans.

I just think it's that these young people live in America—in "the land of the free and the home of the brave"—and they never experienced someone saying, "I love you." It's even more interesting that they had to come to a foreign land to find it, but it's a way God uses, I do believe, just to minister a group of people who were so distracted by the hardships of low self-esteem, and of poor family values…taking them out of their normal surroundings and putting them into a different surrounding where He can really minister to them by the vessels [people] He [God] has over there.

Just by taking them from one situation and moving them to another situation, they are more susceptible to receiving what God has in store for them. In actuality, I look at it as a blessing, because they are empty vessels, young folks and even older folks, who have never been to church at all; but since they are taken out of their normal surroundings and put in this unknown territory, they are more acceptable to what God has in store for them. That opens a door, allowing you to really get in there and be sincere with them, and really minister to them and just fill that empty vessel with the Spirit of God.

Like these young people, being there I too have experienced love, but it's on a different level. Just my love and my faith in God have grown since I've been over there because I've been expecting Him to do great things in the ministry that I'm a part of that's happening over there. So in a sense I can definitely say I can feel His love more there than here because—once again—of all these distractions that we have here.

—J. S. NAVY

Chapter 11

Divorced Mother

*M*Y DEFINITION OF love is God. I say God because I am here, today, living a day before my sixty-fourth birthday because of God's love. And His love has entitled me to live today, and to look forward to living tomorrow. Because of His love, I can have a future; God's love has done that for me.

As a home day care provider, I go about showing love to "little" people, but not only them. I also share love to those I come in contact with. For instance, if I'm in a store and one of the young ladies is waiting on me, and she's got…maybe a scrunched-up face or bad expression, I may go and say, "Hey, Sugar, how you doing?" If she's a teenager, sometimes I'll get a scowl again from her, and then I say, "You know what? I love you today, but most important is Jesus loves you." And then in turn I would get a smile.

In my day care I have some parents who are not saved and have gone through divorce; I might bake a nice little something and share with them or let them take it home. If it's a hot day, I say, "Would you like a glass of lemonade?" I have some Latter-Day Saints who come to my home, and they are sweating bullets. I say, "No, thank you, for whatever you are giving me, but let me give you something." Usually it's a bottle of water. I think that part of me is showing love to other people. I really love people, and I want them to see the light of Jesus in me; so I show love in that manner.

If there is such a feeling that you can get when someone is giving you pockets heavy with gold or money, my heart just seems like it went from a little dark spot to a great big heart that you can probably see illuminated in the sky…Somebody cared enough to pick me out to show me love, and I walk around with this big smile on my face. And if I'm walking, I feel like I'm 10 feet tall instead of 5 foot 3. I walk with an air of anticipation and think, "Can I give this back?" It is such an awesome feeling to feel the love and let that person know who gave it to me just how much it meant to me.

As a divorced mom, I look at the fact that regardless of divorce or whatever, love still can be shown by me, and I feel that love is needed today whether someone is divorced, hurt...or maybe little kids missing their mom when they're gone to work...whatever...I feel more love today is needed, and love is the essence of our being and our connection with God.

You know, when I went through my divorce, I had to still keep showing love. As a matter of fact, I remember one time when I was walking by the nursery, where I and other ladies worked, I overheard two ladies talking bad about me and what I was going through. I was a little bit startled at first, and then the "flesh" just wanted to go back and eat them up, and maybe say some mean things or whatever. But God let the Holy Spirit just come and say to me, "Don't let it go, but go back to address it."

So I went back to them and said, "You two have the audacity to talk about me and what I went through...and the fact that you are pointing your fingers at me...you are pointing four more back at yourself!" I think I showed them love by not going in screaming, but do let them know to be careful, 'cause "if you did that to me, you could very easily do that to someone else, and they may react in a different manner." I think the love was shown because I didn't act the way they would have expected. And I know it was the Holy Spirit dealing with me because at first that was not the way I wanted to react.

Instead of going off on them, I expressed to them how they made me feel. I was wounded, but I did not come out fighting...I came out sharing. I caught them so off guard that their expressions changed; they were so...like in shock, they became each other's face. It was amazing as I saw the transformation as I was speaking to them. I guess here I can say love is also giving correction. It's not always the "feel good" part...that part of love. I know I had to treat them kindly, and not based on what they had done to me.

—SHIRLEY GRATTEER

Chapter 12

The Disc Jockey "DJ"

*M*Y DEFINITION OF love is the feeling of affection you have toward any human being on earth, whether it be a person you are intimately involved with, the person you cross by on the street, the person you have...a feeling of an emotional response.

Well, sometimes I coach at a youth football organization. We have a homecoming every October where I set up my music and play music in between games. That's one way I usually use what I have as love. Also, sometimes people will come up to me and ask, "Hey, can you play this song?" I could be mean and say, "No," 'cause I don't feel like playing it, but I show them a form of affection by saying, "OK...I'll do it for you."

I am very appreciative when I'm shown love. In this world, not a lot of people show that love toward each other. Like I said before, a form of love can just be walking down the street and making eye contact with a person, and saying, "Hey, how are you doing today?" So yeah, I'm very appreciative of it.

I feel good...like I'm a better person...an accomplishment when love is expressed to me. There's nothing better than when you've had a bad day and someone comes up to you and says, "Hey, what's going on?" Sometimes just that "hello" makes you feel better...someone showing a genuine interest in who you are.

I've had the opportunity to express love to people who have never experienced love before. And one of the best ways to show love to someone like that is just doing something kind. If it's a homeless guy, you give him some shoes; when a homeless person sits there, don't just walk by him; say, "Hi, how are you today?" Things like that... The best way to express love to someone who has never experienced it before is to show the act of kindness. Be it somebody you are affectionate

with…just an act of kindness in saying, "How was your day today?"
does more than saying, "Here is a dozen roses."

— "MR. G. Q."

"I Love You"

Faroese	Eg elski teg
Farsi	Tora dost midaram
Filipino	Mahal kita
Finnish	Minä rakastan sinua
Flemish	Ik zie oe geerne
French	Je t'aime
Frisian	Ik hâld fan dei

Chapter 13

Caretaker of Elderly Parents

*M*Y DEFINITION OF love is selflessness. The reason why I say that is because I remember growing up as a child and going to church every Saturday morning. We would usually carry lunch…each family would carry lunch, and we would all gather with our families, then sit and eat together after the main service. My brothers and I were given the awesome task of packing the lunch bag. My mom always made sure that we packed an extra plate, knife, fork, spoon, and cup. Now…we loved to eat! So when mom insisted that we remember to carry extra eating utensils, we never thought that to be a good idea. It meant that we would eventually end up getting less food if someone were to join us for lunch.

We cringed whenever anyone dared come near our section in the lunchroom and hinted that they wanted to join us. My brothers and I had already eyed the largest pieces of chicken in the bowl. We sat as eager children waiting to open long-awaited presents, as we anticipated grabbing at the bowl to pull out the pieces. But that would soon be interrupted by our mother's question to that unwanted guest, "Do you have something to eat? You can join us if you want." As the person sat down, my brothers and I would give each other "the eye" and communicate our displeasure by kicking each other under the table. Gosh! We just hated those moments!

Whether or not she knew someone would join us for lunch, our mom made sure to prepare for it, just in case. She went beyond being reactive. My mom was proactive in her giving. She operated out of selflessness. She taught us to think of others instead of always thinking about ourselves. So to me, that is what love is—being selfless.

I'm a lot like my parents…now. I'm a giver, sometimes ad nauseam. I love to give and believe it is an extension of who I am. When I give, I'm giving a bit of me to someone. And I believe that's the greatest gift you could ever give...yourself, whether it is through a gift, time spent, a gesture...that's who we are. We are people who are conduits through which other people receive. And so, I think I express love by giving.

There is a feeling of warmth that comes over me when someone expresses or shows me love. There are times, however, when I ask, "Why me?" But for the most part I feel really loved...cared for...appreciated. I feel like there are ten million little hands inside of me clapping as if saying, "Yippee! Wow! Really? Oh wow!"

Love... It's just an exciting feeling for me, and I really love it (no pun intended).

By the way...several years later, I found out from our neighbors that they thought we went on a picnic every weekend because we always carried a huge bag with food to church with us on Saturdays. They could not really understand why we were all dressed up for a picnic, but that did not capture their attention as the food bag we carried. Mind you, we also did this while taking public transportation...three buses to be exact.

—EUPHEMIA THOMAS

Chapter 14

Chinese Immigrant and Restaurant Owner

What is your definition of love?

I don't know how to tell you...I don't know this one...my English is not good. In Chinese I tell you, but in English I find hard to say. I know love, but to tell you, it's hard.

How do you show love?

I take family shopping...I go shopping for them. I like looking pretty...doing my hair. I love my husband. I love my son. I like you...I love money (laughing). Sorry...I think I have to go to school for more English.

How do you feel when someone shows you love?

I feel happy! (Smiling)

—SANTAI

"I Love You"

Gaelic	Ta gra agam ort
Georgian	Me shen mikvarkhar
German	Ich liebe Dich
Greek	S'agapo
Greenlandic	Asavakit
Gujarati	Hoo thunay prem karoo choo

Chapter 15

Parent of Special Needs Adult

*M*Y DEFINITION OF love is being with someone who makes you feel like Cinderella; someone who thinks you're beautiful even when you're not; someone who orders chicken fried rice because you like it even though he doesn't; someone who gives you DSW gift cards even though you have too many shoes because he knows you love shoes; someone who stops what they are doing to help you because "your job is always his job"; someone who tells you when you are wrong in a gentle way so you can learn and grow; someone who forgives you when you behave badly and lets it go immediately; someone who makes you feel safe and secure and doesn't use your insecurities against you; and someone who is your best friend.

OK, this is me...explaining my husband's love for me as it makes me love him all the more. But in all seriousness, my definition of love is remembering that God loves everyone and sees the value in each one of us, and that is true love.

I like to think of my life as beginning when I met Lou and Chris—there seems like there was no "before"—it is all there ever was, and it erases all the hurts that are part of the past; it makes all of that seem unimportant. I think of my journey as a love story involving two men, each so much a part of my being that it is difficult to define me anymore without including them in the definition. I am so thankful to God that He created Lou for me and gave him to me as a gift that I am responsible for treasuring and holding dear through life. I do not take for granted the immensity of the present and never disrespect the opportunity to love him and receive his love.

As Chris will tell you, he is my favorite and the one I love best. We have a little game we play:

Chris: "I love you, Amy."

Amy: "I love you too."

Chris: "I love you the most."

Amy: "No, I love you more!"

Chris: "How much?"

Amy: "This much!" as I spread my arms out to their fullest extent and then I say, "And that's more!"

Then we start over again and again and again. My life would be incomplete without his unconditional love and the joy that he brings to my life every day. Being his parent is a blessing that I didn't know I was going to get in life.

How does it make me feel when others show me love? Blessed!

—AMY C.

Chapter 16

Singer and Comedian

*M*Y DEFINITION OF love is an ingredient that, if you manufacture and use it with the right direction—physically, mentally, and spiritually—will help you to really understand. I think it comes with age. As you grow older and meet that special person, you really get a chance to find out more about love. Love is something you have to grow with, and if you accept it, it will stay with you.

I go about showing love through personality. I was so bashful as a kid that I just got a gift for gab. I use humor. I've been blessed with the ability to connect with people of all colors. Some people just don't have a personality, and I've been able to cut through that. Then sometimes you just run into...well, people who are a pain in your...and nobody can help them. But I've always tried to maintain a joyful demeanor.

I'm sixty-six years old, and everybody tells me, "You sure don't act sixty-six...you got a jitterbug walk..." (Laughing). See, I use body language—which I don't do on purpose—but I got that jitterbug walk. I still haven't given up on life, even as bad as the world is now. And I'm always motivating people, which is amazing to me. People come up to me and talk...that's amazing to me 'cause I don't have a PhD.

Experiencing love...It's like a baseball catcher's mitt and glove. It's acceptance to me. It makes you feel good and puts a shell around you where...when the "naysayers" and imps come and want to spoil your day, it just puts a shield around you. Sometimes I have to come back with a fast one, though. My wife sometimes says, "Wow, you are funny...they don't even know you're getting back at them."

So...when I experience love, I feel insulated, appreciated...and it protects me against those times when someone's intent is to hurt me. Love helps to shield me.

—H. BURRELL

"I Love You"

Hawaiian	Aloha wau ia oi
Hebrew	Ani ohevet otcha
	[woman to a man]
	Ani ohev otach
	[man to a woman]
	Ani ohev otcha
	[man to a man]
	Ani ohevet otach
	[woman to a woman]
Hindi	Hum tumhe pyar karte hae
Hopi	Nu'umi unangwa'ta
Hungarian	Szeretlek te'ged

Chapter 17

The Lawyer

*L*OVE IS THE ability to see people at their worst, knowing their life may be of little or no benefit to you and, despite this knowledge, you choose to continue the relationship without expectations. How I go about showing love is by being patient, kind, and without demands.

I've been practicing law now for over a decade, and the more I deal with people, the more I find that there is one key element that is missing—gratitude. Sometimes that challenges my ability to love. I worked for the district attorney's office for a few years and then decided to open my own law firm. Why? Because I wanted to help people, people who more than likely cannot afford expensive lawyers, who sometimes don't really care about themselves or their families— but want excellent service.

I work hard for every client I have. Sometimes they are as guilty as sin, but I still do right by them and try to negotiate for a lesser sentence or for leniency. This is what gets me though…when I've done my best, I get them a good deal, and then they turn around, look me in my face, and start cussing me out. Really! Cussing me out saying, "I want another lawyer … you ain't done your best!" Now mind you, they're guilty! I know they're guilty; they know they're guilty! And everybody in the court knows they're guilty, but they're cussing me out 'cause they don't think they should get any jail time for what they did!

Some even have the nerve to ask me for the retainer fee they paid me. All the work I do…staying up until three and four o'clock in the morning trying to find loopholes or something to give them a second chance or a better deal. I put my family through so much because of the work I do, and then the client turns around and cusses me out. That right there is some ungrateful mess! But you know what? I still get up every morning and go into the office 'cause I know somebody out there who really needs me is going to walk through my doors looking for a good lawyer who will give him more than his money's worth. Maybe this will be the client to show some gratefulness somewhere down the road.

Love plays a big part in what I do to help people 'cause I would have told those ungrateful clients where they could go … and possibly quit the profession by now. But my love for people and wanting to do what I can to help them keeps me going. I appreciate being loved because I know that love is a choice. Hence when a person chooses to love me, I appreciate the gesture.

—A. Thomas

Chapter 18

Special Education Teacher

*L*OVE IS A reaction ... a way you feel about something, someone—your significant other, your husband, your peers.... your dog, your cat ... just someone you have a true passion for. As far as education ... I love education! I think it's the key to success; that's why I continue to equip myself with the necessary tools so that in return I can help others ... help them to be self-sufficient in society.

For example, my students, how I show love is by teaching them the necessary concepts—it doesn't matter what that is—if I'm teaching math, then I show them by writing equations on the board and work with them until they can see it; they hear it because I tell them; I use manipulatives (kinetic pieces), and I use instructions to show them love.

Then of course I tell them, "Good job," and give them a hug. I don't have a problem with doing that ... I give them "thumbs up"; I give them "dap"; whatever it takes ... smiling at them and telling them, "Hey, you're doing good!"... giving them free time, prizes ... For instance, if I know a student likes cars, then I'll get pictures of cars that he can color, or get model cars, and I'll get puzzles of cars so that when it's that student's free time, he can choose whichever activity he wants with the cars.

I take my students on trips and do different activities with them ... but I think the one thing I just love doing is teaching them ... any way I have to teach them. If I have to get on the floor or if I have to stand on the roof and teach them, then I will.

I take them places, and after I've taught them and they actually see and get the concepts, I just enjoy it ... the interaction with my students on a daily basis. And then I just love seeing their faces when they get the concepts. That expression lets me know, "Oh, I got it!" Or "Hey! Thanks, Doc!"

So ... love is just a way of showing or expressing how you feel abou something … that passion that you have. Like I said, education is a passion, as I am a special education educator. That's probably something that God just gave me, the gift to help others, and I just enjoy it—serving my students, and letting them see that, "Hey, I love you all and I'm gonna take the extra time to do what's necessary"—even if they come in with not even a pencil or paper. That's OK 'cause I'm gonna supply everything that they need for school. And I don't have a problem, you know, getting it so they can get it. I just want to share all that I have with my students on a daily basis. I just thank God for the opportunity to be able to empower these students … these special ed students whom no one thought could make it or people just cast aside. God gave me the gift to empower them, and so I do what I do gladly.

When others show me love … honestly, I don't know how to feel because it's not shown that much, outside of my husband. I'm a giver not a taker, so when it's shown, sometimes I don't even know when it's shown. I know that sounds crazy, but whatever it is … I feel happy, elated, and very, very appreciative. When it's genuine, you know it, and you're really grateful to someone for saying it or giving cards or flowers. I feel great! I feel honored!

I don't give love to get love, though. I show love because that's the kind of person I am. I don't do this for this reason so you can do that! No, no…I don't do it for that reason. I just think you should just show love. If you get it back, that's good.

If I do something good for you and you don't do the same thing to me in return, that's not gonna stop me from doing good. But when someone does do good to you, it's just a great feeling.

I will always show love because I think I'm a loving person. I might not get it from that person I show it to, but I'm not gonna stop showing it.

—Shelley D. H.

"I Love You"

Icelandic	ég elska þig
Indonesian	Aku Cinta Kamu
Irish	Taim i' ngra leat
Inuit	Negligevapse
Italian	Ti amo [relationship, lover, spouse]
	Ti voglio bene [Friend or relative]
Japanese	Ai shiteru

Chapter 19

Unemployed Twenty-Three-Year-Old Ex-Offender

Love … it's a feeling … a person that's there … that cares. It's basically caring.

I express it by showing that I care; I offer help … ask if a person needs something … I do things for people … you know … help people out. That makes me feel good. Man … I feel good when I do stuff like that.

Whenever I experience it, it feels good. See, I grew up without any close relatives 'cause they died early. So for me … it makes me feel like I got family again.

— "Mr. Hopeful"

Chapter 20

Retired Construction Worker

*L*OVE IS GROWTH. It's a blessing experience that doesn't hurt. It's a type of sharing that resembles the bounty of nature or the gift of God. You know... Nature is so plentiful. You look at the oil spill ... (chuckling) ... that's a lot of love there too...it just won't stop; they can't cap it. It's not to say the earth is bad, mean, or even evil. That's just the bounty of the earth...the earth that can benefit man.

Love is unconditional...it doesn't hurt. It's what you want to do, but it's a growing thing in this world.

I love to be accepted by people, but there are some people that won't accept me (chuckling). I'm a giver. I love to give. I've learned, "Don't cast pearls to swine," but that's my way of showing love...I love to give. I wanna be the one that's the host. I want to have the goods to give; I want to be the one that accommodates...that's my way of showing love.

My way of showing love is to take the tension off of people to the degree that I'm so connected to creation, the Divine, the Lord, that I have enough that I can give without hurting myself.

It's an honor when love is expressed to me. It's just an honor! Not so much that I may have a wounded self-esteem problem, but it's just an honor because it strengthens the fact that love is a greater force in creation than anything that is mild or negative.

Love actually is the law of nature, the law of creation. We call it love because that's what we were taught, but it's a continuous, ongoing thing in creation. It's the greatest honor in the world. Some people take love for granted maybe because there's no void in them, constitutionally, but there are voids in me. And I know all people have voids 'cause there is something lacking in everybody. And love is so multifaceted that when you get it, it just makes you feel unafraid in creation with elements that may make you feel like a piece of...you know! But love...just when you get it…it enamors you. It just makes you feel so much a part of creation.

That's why it's so important to give love because there may be other areas of life that a person may feel that they're wronged, or there's a situation that's wrong, or people are doing them wrong. So when they get love, it just strengthens them. It makes them more capable of dealing with being here in this life.

—Rob

Chapter 21

Divorced Father

LOVE, IN MY definition, is when one gives of her or himself with no limits or conditions. Love is when that person who you care about...their personal issue becomes an "us" issue. It's where everything stops and you work together to find answers to that "national" issue. Basically, what he or she is battling with becomes important to you.

There are many ways I go about showing love. The one thing that stands out most regarding how I show love is giving. I usually shower the ones I love with gifts or give more of my time. Oh yeah...I also verbally say it and physically show it with hugs, kisses, and favors.

When others portray or show love to me, it makes me feel special and needed. It gives me a feeling of self-worth...and to me, that's a great feeling.

— "MR. SECURITY"

Chapter 22

The Banker

MY DEFINITION OF love is that it is an emotion…it is an action word. You go out of your way to make someone special. All the feelings in the world are balled up in that one word. It is kind of hard to answer that question…because it is an all-encompassing feeling—emotional, physical, spiritual—it is everything all in one that you have for a person. Because of the love you have for the person, all those feelings come forth.

Maybe I don't know what love is! Maybe I haven't experienced it enough in my lifetime…true love that is. Maybe because of life experiences…I haven't experienced it yet. My first response is a textbook answer, so maybe I really don't know. Maybe I don't know about true love because I never knew my father. I never really had a male figure in my life to show me what love is. I guess that's why I have trouble with trusting.

The love that I do know, I show that love by what I do for people. I try to be there for people…being there…in silence, and giving advice when needed.

Sometimes I show love by correcting a wrong, assisting financially. As a banker, I care about people and their money. By making sure they make wise financial decisions with their money, especially for the future, I guess is how I show love.

Teaching people how to save when they are young minimizes the stress that is associated with trying to save money in a shorter period of time as they get older.

When others show me love—at least if I interpret what they are doing as love—it makes me feel like I don't deserve it. I really haven't felt like anyone has really loved me unconditionally, though. I question when someone shows love because I think they have ulterior motives…maybe, besides really having true love for me. Again, as I'm talking with you, I'm beginning to see that some of the issues I have with trusting and understanding love go back to my not having that father in my life who could have helped in all of this. Hmm...this is interesting.

You know, I realize that as a child I just never really belonged anywhere. I wasn't my mom's favorite, and my dad was not there to even make a choice between my sister and me. I look so much like my dad that my mom was never really fond of me either. See...he left my mom for another woman in town just a few years after I was born. I don't know if I have truly dealt with this in a proper way. I go through life doing OK for myself, but there are a lot of wounds that need healing. I guess the love of others has kept me, huh? Yeah! I think so.

—P. Wright

"I Love You"

Kannada	Naanu ninna preetisuuttene
Khmer	Oun Sronlanh Borng
	[to a man]
	Borng Sronlanh Oun
	[to a woman]
Kimeru	Ninkwendete
Konkani	Hanv Tuzo Mog Kortam
Korean	Tangsinul sarang ha yo
Kurdish	Ez te hezdikhem

Chapter 23

Author and Five-Time Cancer Survivor

*M*Y DEFINITION OF love is from a biblical perspective. John 13:34 says, "A new commandment I give unto you, that ye love one another; as I have loved you, that ye also love one another" (KJV). That to me is unselfish love. We need a lot of that around because if we love each other as we love ourselves, we would have fewer quarrels, and we would do things and think about how our actions are going to affect the next person, whether negatively or positively. We would take time out to think of each other if we really practiced unselfish love.

I express love in simple ways…like…it doesn't have to be anything expensive. Like cooking a meal for a friend…going by and helping with whatever…with house chores. Between husband and wife…the husband comes home to a clean house…the wife comes home to a lovely meal cooked by her husband. Give simple gifts not on special occasions…just bringing something or saying, "I love you," or giving a hug; take time out and give the person time…and hold a hearty conversation…

When others show me love, I feel special, I feel loved, appreciated. And as a result of having this special feeling, it gives me the desire to express what I've experienced to the giver and others.

Love brings peace and security.

I went through three different types of cancer five times. My experience causes me to look at love somewhat a little differently, although I was a lovable person before all of that happened. My mom showed us a lot of love as children…I learned from her. She went through some rough times, but you would never have known it because she was such a loving person.

Having survived cancer five times causes me to love even more, be more compassionate and more understanding.

—ALFANCENA MILLICENT BARRETT

Chapter 24

Motivational Speaker

SHOWING APPRECIATION TO others at your own expense without
expecting anything in return—that's what love is. Love is learning
how to quickly forgive and not bring up the past. Having a little
daughter, I truly begin to understand how God loves me. My daughter
can frustrate me one moment, then smile the next, and I will forget
about the frustration. That is how God is with us. We frustrate Him
one moment, but He is right there at the very next moment to love us
some more.

I know that my own love language is affection, but to the people in
my life, I display love by spending quality time and giving gifts. My
wife and daughter experience my love the most. Quality time is very
important to both my wife and daughter. It's hard because it is not as
important to me, but it is to her. That's the tough part about love. It's so
easy to inject selfishness. Even when I don't feel like watching a Lifetime
movie or a cheerleading competition, I sit there with a smile because I
know the time is coming when she will be watching a basketball or
football game.

When love is expressed, it makes you feel appreciated and valued.
Everyone likes to know that other people are thinking about him or
her. It really means a lot when it's shown on a normal day, not just
Father's Day or a birthday. When someone says or does something out
of the blue, it means so much more than it would on a holiday.

—A. JAMISON

Chapter 25

College Student, Wife, and Mother

*M*Y DEFINITION OF love centers in the relationship that I have with my earthly father who stayed with my sister and me for ten years as a single dad and took care of us when he and my mother separated. I center my definition of love around his behavior because it was my first impression of what love really is. It was unconditional, stable, always the same…it was counted on and leaned on just as a security that I found in the fact that he was always there no matter what happened and that he unconditionally loved us. Despite his own hardship, he always managed to be stable for us. I know that was difficult because he hurt many times. Love to me was that…that's exactly what it was: that support and unconditional approval and also the stable, always the same affection for my sister and myself…and sacrifice as well.

As a dad, he had to play the role of a mom and a dad. As little girls we wanted things he couldn't provide for us, but he tried. We wanted ribbons and bows and barrettes—like other little girls—and so because he didn't see any reason for doing all that, he gave us… we had two rubber bands and Vaseline. And so he washed it…washed it good; and shined our hair up with the Vaseline; and we had the two rubber bands and two pigtails and that was it! To him that was it…that provided us a neat little hairstyle, and he was able to take care of us that way.

Another key word for love is sacrifice. That's what he did the whole time. It has to be portrayed…'cause if love is not portrayed, you're not going to know that it's even there. That's why I like to use him as my example 'cause that's what he did. It's got to be put into action and shown; so to me that's how it was shown.

When I portray love to others, I try to make them feel secure, protected, covered…because that's what love does. For instance, when someone is lonely, if someone is hurt, showing love might be by comforting him or her. But at the same time, if someone needs correction or needs rebuke or needs something that I have to confront or deal with, then I might show love by confrontation if that is what is needed at that time.

Portraying love for me is looking for the need and then responding to it in the way that is best for the person—not the way that is most comfortable for me, not the way the person even wants it, but the way that's best for the individual. For instance, children; sometimes love is shown through discipline, sometimes it's in giving them things; sometimes it's refraining from giving them things. So I guess portraying love for me takes on many different facets, but basically it's based on the need of the person as I perceive it.

Love makes me feel secure, protected, covered...just safe. Those are words to show how love makes me feel when it is shown or expressed to me.

—R. B. FRANKS

"I Love You"

Lao	Koi hak jao
Latin	Te amo
Latvian	Es tevi milu
Lebanese	Bahibak
Lithuanian	Aš tave myliu
Luxembourgish	Ech hun dëch gaer

Chapter 26

1960's Riot Survivor

*M*Y DEFINITION OF love is…well, that question takes me back…back to the good old days. Love is looking out for people. Back then we looked out for each other 'cause we had to survive. It blows my mind today when you hear people say, "I don't care what so-and-so is doing…or what's happening with so-and-so."

I remember when I worked for GC Murphy (a five-and-dime store) in the mid-1960s…before the riots broke out in Washington DC. If we were lucky enough to have chicken or roast beef dinner over the weekend, and knew a "sister" was coming to work without food, we would carry an extra sandwich. Another would bring juice or something else to give to a "sister" who didn't have anything. Many of the "sisters" who worked at GC Murphy migrated from Virginia, Mississippi, Pennsylvania, and Georgia 'cause DC was a place of opportunity. Times were hard then. We knew some of them weren't from the area…they would work and send money back home to their families and all. They shared rooms in boarding houses. And so we did what we could to help people out.

When the riots actually happened, I didn't know Martin Luther King Jr. was killed. I was leaving to go grocery shopping that morning. I got into the Giant Foods Store on the 14th Street Corridor. I had a few things in my cart when suddenly there was this rush…a stampede of people came running into the store…then out of nowhere the glass to the store broke and a car exploded! Someone threw a Molotov cocktail.

The manager, a white man, looked at me and said, "Keep the stuff in your cart…take whatever you want…take the cart…be careful…look out for glass… and get out of here…go now!" I remember running out of the store with the cart. I was so afraid… I didn't stop running with the grocery cart 'til I got home…nine blocks away. I don't even remember what route I took to get home…all I know is I was scared.

Looking back…that was a terrible time for me and my children…for that matter, everybody. But you know what? It didn't change me…it didn't change a lot of us…we still knew people mattered.

How do I show love? Well…with me personally, as a better Christian, I try to reflect God's love by lending a hand, I do volunteer work for the Smoky Mountain Children's Home in Tennessee, I prepare dinner for folks who are sick in my church, and I am the liaison between the Fifty and Over Club and the younger generation. There is so much you can do just because you are a child of God.

When other people express or show me love…hmm. I know this…I know my works don't get me into heaven…(pauses and sniffs with tears coming down face)…but I know how it feels when you are in need…or when you're down in the dumps, and someone comes along… and says a word, gives you a hug, or gives you something to eat. That right there is a good feeling…yeah…a good feeling. It does matter, you know!

—MOMMA SHIRLEY

"I Love You"

Macedonian	Te sakam
Malayalam	Njan ninne premikkunnu
Malaysian	Saya cintakan mu
Maltese	Inhobbok
Mandarin	Wo ai ni
Mohawk	Kanbhik
Maori	Kei te aroha au i a koe
Marathi	Maaze tuzhyavar prem ahe
Moroccan	Kanhebek
Navaho	Ayor anosh'ni
Norwegian	Jeg elsker deg

Chapter 27

Success Strategist

I USED TO THINK that love was a word that should only be used after I've explained what was meant by my usage to an individual, especially in my dating circle days. However, after learning and maturing in understanding relationships, I define love simply as being in a posture of giving. Love is based on the giver and not the recipient. True love does "in spite of" not "because of."

I now understand that love cannot be portrayed or shown unless one has experienced it. It is through my understanding, experience, and fellowship with the Creator of love that I am now able to show love through my interest in others' goals and dreams, in listening twice as much as talking, and not allowing what others do to affect the way I love.

Based on my current definition of love, I have a feeling of warmth and value when shown love. It also let's me know that the giver has had an experience with love him or herself. Love, without strings attached, is a wonderful thing.

—AL PEARSON

Chapter 28

The Receptionist

LOVE IS PATIENT. That's my definition of love.

If you love somebody, you have to be patient with them...you can't want them to be the way you want them to be when they are already who they are. So you gotta be patient because people try to change people, but you can't change people. People have to change their own self or God has to change them. So if you love them, you're going to compromise with them, and if they have some ways that may be compromising...well then you have to be strong about that... and just keep supporting them on their negative way or just pray about it. I believe in prayer, so that is why I choose love and can talk about love.

If I have a problem with someone and I know that they may not love me...I look beyond that. For example, if I'm working as a receptionist and someone calls on the phone, and I introduce myself...by the time I say my name, he may not want to speak to me, and hangs up the phone in my ear. But because of my love, if he calls back, I will continue to treat him professionally, because that's my love and compassion, and that's how I demand my respect from him. If he continuously does this and I continuously treat him professionally, he's the one who's going to stop and wonder why. He's the one who's going to feel guilty...but I don't have to feel guilty anymore because I make my path clear. I don't have to walk around with a heavy burden any more because it's off my chest.

When you show love, it makes you happy. It does! At least that's how I feel.

—S. ANTHONY

Chapter 29

Sexually Abused Female

I DON'T HAVE ONE definition of love. It has had different definitions for different stages in my life. At this time in my life I would define love as having someone to love and that someone loving you back. I am learning that love does not have a face and must be given with kindness and unselfishly.

It depends on whom I am showing it [love] to, for what purpose, and what type of love the circumstance requires [when I show love].

How does it make me feel when others show me love? It depends on what others call showing love. I've had people tell me they love me and then abuse me, abandon me, and use me.

—J. BYRD

"I Love You"

Pashto	Za stha sara meena kawoma
Persian	Man ashegheto hastam
Pilipino	Mahal kita
Polish	Kocham Cie
Portuguese	Amo-te
Punjabi	Mai taunu pyar karda
Romanian	Te iu besc
Russian	Ya tyebya lyublyu

Chapter 30

Professional Makeup Artist

$\mathcal{M}$Y DEFINITION OF love is having compassion for yourself and others, but love is something of a connection between seeing God in another person, seeing life and love is being attracted to your opposite...anything that is your opposite. Like if I see a flower and say, "Oh, I love that flower," or love is in beauty and compassion.

As a makeup artist, I show love with compassion. I take a moment and connect with someone's eyes and make an assessment of what kind of person I am dealing with, and then I continue with giving love through taking the time to come up with a color...a beautiful image in my mind; then I'm able to apply it to their face...then they look in the mirror and say, "How did you do that? What did you do?" From now on I think I'm going to say, "I put love into it!"

Some of the people I've worked on....hmm...I go from Queen Noir to Queen Latifah. I've done eight, maybe nine world leaders; the last six presidents. I've worked with Vladimir Putin, I've done Abdullah Abdullah, and I've worked with the whole Senate and have done Nancy Pelosi as well as members of the Republican National Committee.

I keep love in my heart wherever I go and don't try to be one side or the other. Love plays into my life because of polarity. Since I was a little girl—my mother is of one background and my father is of another...that is very opposite polarity—I've had to learn to deal with bringing opposites together.

One of my favorite people to work on was Joan Rivers, and the quickest and funniest—if I'm going to be in the comedy world—was Jon Stewart. And I've worked on a lot of the *Politically Incorrect* shows with Bill Maher; and before that it was Dennis Miller.

Speaking of love...they have such a passion and love for making sure that people see both sides...making sure people know what's really going on. That has, in the past fifteen years, been an incredible career for Bill Maher (some may be a bit outspoken, but they're able to, in their own little way, show their love of politics).

(Laughing) You're not supposed to talk about religion and politics, but I'm always talking about religion and politics...Colin Powell is my favorite! I liked working with Charlton Heston...he was hilarious. He just wanted to get in the chair and get out! I said to him once, "Did you do those movies when they took hours to do your makeup?" Then he goes, "That's exactly why I want to get out of this chair!" Then after I did his makeup, I said, "I just did Moses's makeup...I'm so excited!"

I love working with Hillary Clinton because she connects with you; I've worked with her husband, Bill Clinton, and he *totally* connects with you. He connects with you on a visual, physical level 'cause physically his eyes make contact with yours...he really connects with you. I think Hillary connects with you in a way where it's deeper...its more with just in the moment. She's a very "in the moment person"...get it done! ...and Bill's kinda like...really goes in deep.

So going full circle to when I told you about how do I give love when I'm doing or putting love into my work...it really is being considerate, and it is being aware and it is being appropriate with respect to their time, but it's also to use my gift to look at a face and "accentuate the positive and get rid of the negative."

I can keep talking if you let me, but...when love is expressed or shown to me, I feel like a hummingbird...like a little bit of energy and lifted and beauty and elation. I also feel a comfort.

—MICHELE MARCELLO

Chapter 31

Grandmother

*M*Y DEFINITION OF love is family, caring, discipline, being "touchy-feely," and giving words of affirmation.

I portray love by showing others respect, offering much prayer for others, and caring.

I grew up without love, so it is very difficult to accept when it's being shown to me, but I'm learning. I sometimes wonder what motives are attached to it. When it comes, I feel a bit awkward and wonder, "What do you want?"

Like I said before, I'm still learning how to accept love. Granted, I love giving it, but I have trouble accepting it. I love my children and my grandchildren, but I'm still learning how to accept it from others.

—W. MYERS

Chapter 32

The Accountant

*M*y definition of love is unconditional acceptance. When I think about love, it should be a holistic acceptance of the person in terms of their strengths as well as their weaknesses. When you love someone, you should be accepting of all aspects of him or her, not just the parts that are beneficial to you.

I realize more now than ever that, in the body of Christ, I see love transitioning into a self-centeredness…an evolving is taking place where relationships are now being based on what someone can get rather than on what someone give. I see friendships being degenerative—people hooking up with people to jockey for positions…and as they move up, they connect with people for the wrong reasons.

I read a book a couple years ago that really impacted me—*The Five Love Languages* by Gary Chapman. I found out that everybody has a love language, and it comes about based on how they were raised. I found out that my love language—the way I show love—is through affirmation. I need that to feel love; whereas my husband, he needs face time.

My way of showing love is by talking and listening without being judgmental. I don't have a lot of friends, so I am pretty discretionary with what I share with people 'cause you can't tell everybody everything…because they'll use it against you at some point.

I find that the older I get, the harder it becomes to stay connected with people you care about because you get so caught up with being busy. I don't want to look around one day and realize that this person is gone. I recognize that I've not been as careful with staying in touch because of my responsibilities.

You know…when I look back on some of the friendships I've had, my greatest hurt came from females and leaders in the church who I trusted. I didn't grow up in church, so I always have a high expectation of leaders and people in the body of Christ. I never expected to experience certain behaviors and see certain things…but I have now come to realize that life happens. I have faced betrayal and a lack of reciprocation in relationships, sometimes from people I've been in the trenches with…people who I've joined in spiritual warfare and battles. And then come the betrayal and the rejection!

The interesting thing is that I have to use caution and make sure that I don't operate based on my wounded feelings, but let God come in and take all of that…and then be able to show true love no matter what…although I'm still a bit guarded at times. Sometimes I wonder if folks who call me their friend truly feel that way because they genuinely care for me or if they are seeking to get something from me. True friendship is very rare…really.

In my profession as an accountant—which I do in a secular sense and as ministry—I show love by showing people how to manage their income. However, the greatest way I show love is not to judge them, because a lot of time people have high levels of education but don't know how to manage their finances. But that's their weakness— they just don't know how to handle finances—it's not that they have problems mentally or are not intelligent. I think they appreciate the fact that I don't judge them but try to help them with change through technical teaching. That's the way I do it with clients and even my staff.

I feel appreciated and valued when I experience love. I think that's the biggest thing 'cause I think that's what I look for. As I said before, my love language is words of affirmations…so, yeah…I guess I do look for appreciation and…I guess validation. That's what I feel when I'm shown love.

Are we supposed to get all that from God? Maybe so, but at the same time I think that thinking that way restricts us from the connectivity of the "body" because I think we should look for appreciation from those who are colaboring with us. I don't think it should be like you should never expect…or resolve in your mind, "Don't show me no appreciation!" No! I think a mature Christian does appreciate being valued by others.

—A. D. GOODRICH

"I Love You"

Samoan	Ou te alofa ia te oe
Sardinian	Ti kerio meta
Serbian	Volim te / Lubim te
Setswana	Ke a go rata
Sindhi	Maa tokhe pyar kendo ahyan
Singhala	Mama oya'ta a'darei
Sioux	Techihhila
Slovak	Milujem Ťa
Slovenian	Ljubim te
Somalian	Waan ku gealahay
Sotho	Ke a o rata
Spanish	Te amo
Srilankan	Mam Oyata Arderyi
Swahili	Naku penda (followed by the person's name)
Swedish	Jag älskar dig
Swiss German	Ich lieb Di

Chapter 33

Mechanic and Home
Improvement Contractor

Love. I can tell you I know love. I've been there...I know love (laughing). Love is a high...(Laughing)...makes you levitate...let me put it that way! Levitate is floating...floating out your body...for me that's what love is.

How do I go about showing love? Hmm...let me see...well, most people do the hook, line, and sinker. I do the boat, the dock, and everything when I show love. Basically, I give my all in all in the love thing. It's a good thing...it's a love high. My high is music, life...and other things...you know... (Laughing).

I feel beautiful when love is expressed to me...I don't like to be tricked with love, though. Love has to be a two-way street, not one-way. I want things as they are...no tricks!

—J. B. L. "JACK OF ALL TRADES"

Chapter 34

The Psychologist

*W*HOA! THESE ARE some serious questions and challenging to put into words.

Well, I could go on forever with this question, but simply put, my definition of love is having, showing, and sharing genuine attunement toward another being.

I feel as if I show love by genuinely caring for another being. That love and care for another being may be expressed in so, so many different ways: some overt, some not so overt. For example, doing something for that being that helps them or helping that being do something for themselves that helps them—teaching, feeding, assisting, listening, caring, acknowledging, etc.—is showing love. Some less overt ways of expressing love might be praying for that being or consciously sending them loving energy.

Love can be shown in so many different ways. Sometimes even a genuine smile or eye contact, acknowledging—and not looking "through"—another living being, whether you know them or not, is a powerful expression of love for humankind, I think.

It has been through my professional experience that I have become more aware of and realized that, sadly, many beings in this world feel invisible. From personal experience, I know it is painful to feel invisible, and the fact that so many beings experience this hurts my heart; thus, my feeling that the genuine acknowledgement of another being can be an expression of love holds true.

It feels really nice to experience love. Thanks to my education, I recently became aware that there is a warm energy that swirls around my heart when I am shown love or have the fortunate opportunity to show love to another being. Having love shown to me feels comforting and safe and also provides that much needed sense of belongingness.

—R. BERTRAM

"I Love You"

Tagalog	Mahal kita
Tahitian	Ua here vau ia oe
Taiwanese	Wa ga ei li
Tamil	Naan unnai kadhalikiraen
Telugu	Nenu ninnu premisthunnanu
Thai	Chan rak khun [to a man]
	Phom rak khun [to a woman]
Tonga	Ndakuyanda
Tunisian	Ha eh bak
Turkish	Seni seviyorum
Turkmen	Men seni söýýan

Chapter 35

The Pastor

OVE. LOVE IS sacrificing yourself for someone else…giving of yourself…giving your total being. In other words, you put the other person first. When there are things that you possibly would want to do or to have for yourself, you put yourself second and you give to the other person.

I go about showing love by doing just that! I don't always show love (laughing), but when I show love, it's definitely when I really don't necessarily feel like doing something, giving something…when I just really feel like being me. But I just put me aside and say to myself, "What's best for the other person?" and I give and do for someone else when I would rather be doing for myself or not doing at all.

As a pastor, there are a lot of times you don't feel like doing your pastoral duties, especially when doing things for people whom you know who don't necessarily receive it or who really don't care that much for you personally. Yet at the same time you are, I would say, obligated or commanded to do those duties in spite of and regardless of what they are going to do or say about you or about it; still you do it anyway.

A lot of times you don't necessarily feel like taking the time to even pick up the phone to say something kind or send a kind e-mail. Sometimes you just would rather do something else, but you know that you really need to take the time to let this person know that you are thinking of them and to encourage them. And there are times when you do things for people who have hurt you, said things about you, or whatever. But you do the right thing regardless of what they've done, what they said…you still do the right thing.

That obligation is there for anyone, but as a pastor, you have been called to go beyond…let's say beyond the ordinary person. You have been called to certain duties. For example, you're called to take a lot of time, let's say, with a person. First of all, they come to you because you are a pastor, and they bring certain things to you, certain situations. A lot of times they may be very hurtful situations; they're confiding in you, and you take time with them to walk with them through it, and even though later they may stab you in the back, you don't divulge the secrets and the things that you know about them; you continue to hold it.

There are things that I will hold until the Lord takes me out of here! Even though the same people have "stabbed me in the back," so to speak, and they've hurt me, yet I'm not going to tell what I know about them...I'm gonna keep it. And that's love! Love is covering a multitude of sin. Yes, love covers.

I feel very good when people show me love, but I've not always felt that way. There were times when people were more than likely showing me love, but I couldn't receive it because sometimes I was concerned about the motive of that person...whether they were really doing this because they really want to show me love or they are doing it because they can benefit or receive from it. And then there have been some times when I think I wasn't worthy of whatever it was they were showing me. So, no, I haven't always felt good about someone showing me love.

And then there times when I didn't really know what love was, and that love was what they were really trying to show me. So therefore I wasn't able to necessarily feel good about it or what they were trying to do for me. However, now that I have a better understanding, it does feel good when people show me love, when they sacrifice themselves, and when they go out of their way to even say nice things...'cause people really don't have to be nice to you. They really don't have to say kind things, but when they do, regardless of the motive, still it's better than saying something evil.

Well, the reason why I used to question people's motives...well especially as a younger person...especially with men (laughing)...they have all kinds of motives of showing what could or could not be love. So you have to weigh these things and say, "OK, is this love...and if it is love, why? Is it so I can reciprocate?" So I think that's out of just being cautious and making sure that it's pure. This caution comes from basic human nature; other times it comes from just knowing that people have a tendency to do those things to get what they want.

I don't really question anymore because I don't see it necessary to go through those processes. Either you love me or you don't! I'm going on to tomorrow. Tomorrow the sun's going to rise…it's not a big deal anymore.

—C. F. C.

"I Love You"

Ukrainian	Ja tebe kokhaju
Urdu	May ap se pyar kerthy ho [to a man]
	May ap se pyar kertha ho [to a woman]
Uzbek	Men sizni sevaman
Vietnamese	Aim ew ang [to a man]
	Ang ew aim [to a woman]
Welsh	Rwy'n dy garu di
Xhosa	Ndiyakuthanda
Yiddish	Ikh hob dikh lib
Yoruba	Mo ni fe
Zulu	Ngiyakuthanda

Chapter 36

Retired Civil Servant

*L*OVE IS PATIENCE and kindness. If you don't have patience, you're not going to have love. That's what I deal with since I had my leg amputated. I had to have love and patience…I found out that was the only way.

I feel good…I feel really good when someone shows me love and kindness. I treat people as I want to be treated…that's how I was brought up by my mother. "Treat people like how you want to be treated; if you see a stranger on the street…if you can help him, help him," my mother would say. The elderly people and children are people I help 'cause they can't help themselves. I want my work to be done on earth!

When I had my leg amputated and had to go to the rehab center…I experienced love. The nurses came around me like they were angels and told me it was going to be alright. Even the doctor who worked on my leg said it was going be alright. I didn't have any clothes 'cause I went from one hospital to another. My doctor and some of the nursing staff went out and bought me clothes so I could exercise on my leg so I could get it stronger. Every day they were by my side asking me how I felt and telling me not to worry because everything was going be alright, and that I was going to walk again.

That gave me hope. I used to sit around in the hospital room and cry. I said, "Lord, how am I going to do this?" But then something would come over me and say, "You're a strong woman…you can do it!" If you believe in faith and you get backed against a wall, He said His angels would come around and pull you and say, "Get up…don't stay against that wall…you have to get up…you're going to walk again!"

There's was one time…I didn't know how I was going to pay my rent as I was working and I was doing [everything] by myself, and didn't know how I was going to make it. But my coworkers came around and gave me money to pay my rent for two months. Friends would buy me food…'til I got my supplement check going. My rental lady…she said, "I'll wait on you 'til you get your income tax and then bring your rent up-to-date."

Now I look back and wonder how I got this far. It was only by the good Lord helping me. He knows I am a good person and I would do that for anybody who was in need and couldn't help themselves…I would help people.

I show love by helping other people; telling the story about what I had gone through, and that if you believe, the same will happen for you. You have to try Him…the good Lord…you have to try Him.

I used to play with Him before I got sick. What I mean about "play" is I believed, but I really didn't believe in what He could do. And then when I came in need, I said, "Lord, how is it I'm gonna do this?" He didn't come when I wanted Him to come, but He came right on time, when I really needed Him. I'm telling you and everybody, "Just try Him and you'll see…you'll see."

I had lost my only son, Kevin, to murder just a few years ago. I sat there one night and said, "He's not gone…he's still with me." But the things I remember about him…are the good times… (Smiling) Like…he would come in the house and say, "Ma, you ain't no fun…I'm going down the street!" At other times I would remember when he would say, "Ma, you know I don't eat meat loaf…I eat chicken." I live in the good times…to me he was a good child, and I loved him to death.

When I was on the operating table to get my leg cut off, I saw my uncle and my brother, who are dead, and they said, "You got some more work to do; we're not ready for you yet." And then they turned their backs and walked away from my bed into a dark room. But I didn't see Kevin. I said he was probably running around heaven messing with the Lord, saying, "Oh, she didn't come…she sent the leg, but she didn't come." (laughing) "Yep, she sent her leg, but she didn't come!"

Going through Kevin's death…I sometimes felt bitter, but then I had to change and respond out of love, even though they haven't solved his murder yet. But love keeps me going…it keeps me going.

—Ms. Ella

Chapter 37

The Orator

*M*Y DEFINITION OF love is self-sacrifice. I could give you a tradition or biblical response like...God is love. But think about it... what "was" God? Yep! He was sacrificial... giving up of Himself. So that's why I say love is self-sacrifice.

It may sound like an oxymoron, but it's a giving up of yourself...it is just that! When I think about it, though, I remember the story of Abraham and Isaac. Abraham was ready to give up his son—the child of promise that would make him a father of nations. He did it out of love, and he did it because he trusted.

Giving. This is how I show love...through the gesture of giving. To me—and without beating around the bush—to love someone is to give.

Love is a trust, also...it really is. Although some people abuse it, love is still a trust. God told women to respect men, and men to love women.

Love...it is an indescribable emotion that you want to give to another person or thing.

Having two children is my way of showing love. My grandsons, who are six and four, call me "Grandma Nana." One day I asked them, "Why do you call me 'Grandma Nana'?"

"Why we call you 'Grandma Nana'?"

"Yes, why do you call me 'Grandma' and 'Nana'?" I asked.

"Don't you know?" they snickered.

"No!" I responded.

"Because we love you twice! That's right, Grandma Nana...we love you twice!"

I had no words after that response.

How do I feel when love is shown to me? Ecstatic. Exhilarated. Safe.

—KATHY HAZZARD

Chapter 38

The Social Worker

*I*N A VERY simplistic way, love is an emotion, but it is so much more than that. ...I mean in the Bible it says to love your neighbor. I don't think that means you need to walk up and say, "I love you, man," to every person you see on the street. But I think...there is this feeling that that we are all connected, and love is what connects us all...that we were all created in love and that we exist through love and grace...and they are all connected.

And, of course, there are different kinds of love and stuff like that. But there's a feeling that I care about this person or this other thing...I say "thing" 'cause people love animals as well...and that you care about something and that it means something to you. And so I don't think we use that word enough...you know what I mean? Because I think that is something we should talk more to our children about...I think we would have a better world if we would talk more to our children about love.

You know it's funny, 'cause I always think about the Bible whenever I think about love, though. I'm not like this overly religious person, though I am a believer, but I'm very scattered with my churchgoing. But something I've been thinking about a lot lately is when Jesus made His summation of the laws...and He said the first law is to love God, and the second is to love your neighbor as yourself. And I think people sometimes translate that or think about that, "Oh, it's this thing"...the emphasis is just "Love your neighbor! Love your neighbor!" But I think for me the emphasis is "as yourself."

And I think in this world and as a social worker—I see this a lot— that if you are a person who is broken or fragile, and you do not love yourself...it's real easy to treat other people like they are nothing! It is...it really is because you don't love yourself; so you are treating your neighbors as you love yourself!

And so I think the thing is that...I got into social work...I was a little worried at first because I'm because I'm not a super-extroverted person. I really enjoy being by myself (bursts out with laughter)...but you know what I love about people? I love the humanity...that each of us has joys...we each have sorrows in our life...we all have people who will die on us...we will all have people who move in and out of our lives...we will all have moments where we just laugh and laugh and laugh...

Most people, except the most hardened people, really like children and want them to do well. It's really hard to not like a child or a small animal...and so I think that when I became a social worker, it wasn't like, "Oh...I have to save everybody...I have to help everybody." It was really about, "I want to have a life that is full of people I love and who love me." I think that every other person deserves that too. I think that every person deserves the chance to go to school, and I think that every person deserves to grow up in a home that is violence-free. So I work...I show love because I believe every human being deserves that...and I think that is really loving your neighbor as yourself...that every person deserves this chance.

And part of taking care of your neighbor is knowing that every person should be respected, and every person has a right to live a life full of dignity and to have opportunities to form relationships...to love people and to have whatever a fulfilling life means to them. And so through my work and through social work, I can help create—because it is about social justice—those things too are about love and are about creating opportunities and access for people.

You know it's funny... (Chuckling) I think there is a struggle with sometimes being kind to yourself. Yalom, a psychotherapist who does a lot of existential psychology, talks about the idea that there is a difference between pity and compassion— that pity has an essence about it that is condescending... It's this, "I feel really sorry for you, but thank God it's not me...there is somehow a difference between us because what happened to you is probably your own fault, and I feel sorry for you."

Compassion is more an acknowledgement that we're really not so different, and that if I was in the same situation that you are in right now, I probably couldn't have done anything differently. And because

I am a human being, it may be that I am a different race than you are…I'm a different gender than you…I'm a different age than you, but I am a human being. And so I can understand a piece—not your exact experience—but because I've experienced joy and sorrow and loss…I can have an inkling of what you are going through and I can connect with you. And I think that, working from that premise, and believing that to your being…I'm able to connect with people.

I'm a white woman from the suburbs, but yet I think that you can really connect with people to where they feel that you are yourself, and you can say, "Tell me what you're going through…tell me, because I am a human being…"

I think sometimes it's kind of difficult for me to accept love. I'm used to being in the role that sometimes when people are compassionate with me, I am a little taken aback because I don't know what to do with it. Sometimes I have to remind myself to be kind to myself. And yet I think sometimes when I'm with my family, we have a wonderful time together…it's just unbridled joy, sometimes just laughing…stupid, stupid stuff. It's so freely giving and taking—love going back and forth—that you can't help but have this lightness…this feeling of lightness about yourself. But sometimes it is hard to accept and embrace love.

Romantic love is a whole different thing (snickers)…because it's hard to be vulnerable; it's hard for anyone to be vulnerable and to open yourself up to family, because you can experience rejection and other things with your family as well.

I think when my mom died…the thing I know that's missing the most is…as much as I love my sisters and we have a very mutual relationship, and I know they'd do anything for me—but my mom was like the source of this pure unconditional love. I mean, she wouldn't always come to my rescue, but she was always there radiating that…and to know that this person is not there… She didn't solve all my problems; she didn't send me money or anything like that, but she was always there…and then that made me realize just how much I miss my maternal grandmother, who also died…

I have a really good friend…he's a man, and we won't ever be more than just really good friends…. I think there is something so special about this friendship because there is such reciprocity that it's just really special. Certainly we have things in common and we like doing certain things together, but just the silliness…there's this comfortableness that is so amazing…and how precious that is to me. It is very much a grounding force, I think…

So, yes, although it's difficult to accept sometimes, there is a special feeling that I experience when love comes to me.

— A ROSE AMONG THORNS

Afterword

*L*OVE. WOW! WHAT a powerful word of expression and action. I hope you were overwhelmed by love as you read this book. Have you realized that in today's society some people are overwhelmed by themselves? They will pass by a homeless person and not even look at him or her or even say "Hello!" Some will even bump into you while walking on the sidewalk or rushing to get into the shorter line at the supermarket and not say, "Excuse me." Better still, some will even see you crying at a bus stop and look the other way without saying, "Ma'am, are you OK?" Has society become so crystallized in selfishness that the other person does not matter?

For the most part, we can probably agree that the prevailing terms that resonated with many as they answered the question, "How do you feel when love is shown or expressed to you?" are *happy, special, valued,* and *appreciated.* The testimonies here defy what some members of society have forgotten... they have forgotten to love.

Why does it seem that some of us have forgotten about love? Is it because we, at some level, are afraid to become vulnerable? Shying away from vulnerability is natural. Sometimes I think that if we were to show love to a stranger or even to someone with whom we are familiar, we would somehow feel that we are exposing some level of weakness that we too have and do not want revealed. But why is that?

"No matter what cultural, ethnic, or religious backgrounds we come from, intrinsically we are taught to be independent of others, and not to expect people to do for us what we ought to do for ourselves."[1] So then, is showing love a reminder of what we do not want to become—a person in need—or someone who finds joy in helping another? "In this vulnerability there is a choice... hide our weakness, or embrace it with humility and allow it to become that special place in which to have an encounter with God."[2]

Every one of us was born with the capacity to love. That is our place of vulnerability, as it is not contingent on the response we anticipate, but a need that another has. Yes, we have struggles, and we have our own individual pain, but we need to realize that we have been touched by a part of God that is found within each of us. Somewhere in our journey of life, someone has shown us love. It may have been a kind word or gesture...or maybe just a hug when we needed it most, but we have all experienced some facet of love.

Every person—rich or poor, educated or illiterate, free or incarcerated, able-bodied or handicapped, hopeful or hopeless—deserves our love. There is greatness in all of us, and maybe...just maybe that love shown will awaken a creativity hidden within; encourage a soul to not give up on life; deter the next crime; push a person to write his or her first book; prevent the next suicide attempt; give a second chance to one who has no more chances left; provide comfort to a grieving relative; strengthen a weak patient; provide laughter to someone who suffered a stroke; give friendship to that incorrigible youth; and the list can go on and on...

Your business is life...and life is urgent.

—LUKE 9:60

Christ said this to His disciples just before He entered Jerusalem to show the loudest expression of love—death on a cross. There He would show that true love gives...gives of itself to others with no regrets. His encouragement provided the backdrop that His disciples would need to conduct any and every business in life with urgency—love.

So for you and me...we need to be in the business of life, living our lives with a level of urgency, because maybe today is our or someone else's last time this way. Love is so much a part of life, that to live without it makes us poorer than a pauper with a penny.

Whitney Houston sang the song, "Saving All My Love for You." Well, the time to spend that love has come!

It's time to live out loud!

It's time to laugh out loud!

It's time to love out loud!

We must fight, then, the urge to be self-seeking and embrace selflessness—where life is not about us—and be drawn toward that which will bring happiness, hope, joy, forgiveness, and affection to another.

Ah ... love.

> This is the kind of love we are talking about—not that we once upon a time loved God, but that he loved us and sent his Son as a sacrifice to clear away our sins and the damage they've done to our relationship with God. My dear, dear friends, if God loved us like this, we certainly ought to love each other. No one has seen God, ever. But if we love one another, God dwells deeply within us, and his love becomes complete in us—perfect love!
>
> —1 JOHN 4:10–12

This truth, spoken by John, reveals something wonderful ...

- To love people is to love God.

- To love God is to love people.

- To show love is to show God.

- To experience love is to experience God.

We are very much a part of God's nature ... a divine piece of God that, when put together, we become His arms, His eyes, His feet, and His heart to those who lack His presence in their everyday lives.

Let us make life our business by showing love to others; in doing so, we introduce God to the world.

So go ahead ... love out loud!

After all, it is ... *The Most Important Word.*

Notes

FOREWORD
1. "My Tribute" by Andraé Crouch. Copyright © 1971 Bud John Songs, Inc., admin. EMI Christian Publishing. Permission requested.

AFTERWORD
1. Hewlette A.C. Pearson, "Encountering God in Vulnerability", *The View From the Mountain: The Process of Destiny* (Xulon Press, 2007).
2. Ibid.

About the Author

THE SECOND OF four children born to Felix and Gretel Pearson, Hewlette grew up in a household of love, faith, and much laughter. A native of Kingston, Jamaica, Hewlette immigrated to the United States with her family and took up residency in Washington DC. Thanks to the support of her parents and three brothers, she has accomplished much both in the religious and secular fields. Hewlette has traveled within the United States and overseas to speak to audiences about the hope that is found in Christ Jesus, and to encourage and empower today's generation for the next level. She is a vivacious, common sense, down-to-earth speaker who possesses a sense of humor that captivates audiences wherever she goes.

Hewlette has earned master's degrees from Johns Hopkins University in Baltimore, Maryland, and Regent University in Virginia Beach, Virginia. She is also a member of Phi Delta Kappa, an international fraternity of educators, and is listed in Who's Who Historical Society's 2001–2002 *International Who's Who of Professional Educators*. She has also studied abroad at Oxford University, England, completed religious study tours in Greece and Italy, and is a frequent workshop presenter at conferences.

She is a member of the ministerial staff at The Gateway to Wholeness Church Ministries in Largo, Maryland, and is the director of the church's In Pursuit of His Presence Worship Institute, emphasizing worship in the art of dance, mime, flags, banners, and praise and worship ministry.

Hewlette published her first book in 2007, *The View From the Mountain: The Process of Destiny,* which speaks of struggles and triumphs encountered on the path to destiny and lessons learned along the way. She has also has written articles for magazines and co-authored a publication.

Currently, she travels to speak empowering messages to audiences of different ages and backgrounds, and to promote her books. She also puts her ministry-teaching gift to use as founder of Mind Over Matter Empowerment Center, where she provides "lifestyle makeover" and job-readiness skills training to ex-offenders. For over seven years, Hewlette has provided education, motivation, and hope to at-risk populations. She works with youth and adults in the juvenile and adult justice systems, as God has given her a passion for this often neglected and misunderstood population.

As Hewlette continues to minister the gospel and to share her life experiences with youth and adults, her desire is to bring hope and joy to those in need. It is without fail that people leave her presence empowered to live life the way God intended—freely. The call of God upon her life was birthed out of the Scripture: *"God's Spirit is on me; he's chosen me to preach the Message of good news to the poor, Sent me to announce pardon to prisoners and recovery of sight to the blind, To set the burdened and battered free, to announce, 'This is God's year to act!'"* (Luke 4:18–19).

Hewlette has been blessed with many gifts and talents with which to reach the nations; however, she believes strongly in being led by the Holy Spirit in every aspect of her life. For Hewlette, ministering to others is her gift, but God is her passion.

About Andraé Crouch

ANDRAÉ CROUCH IS without question one of the most vital and influential artists in contemporary music today. His artistry has touched and changed millions of lives around the world. An international music star of legendary stature, he transcends color, class, and creed with a vibrant message of hope, faith, and joyous celebration.

There has always been a great deal of anticipation and unpredictability surrounding the gospel legend and pastor of the New Christ Memorial Church of God in Christ in San Fernando, California. For more than two decades he has forged a multifaceted career as world-class recording artist, songwriter, arranger, and producer. He has worked with a cavalcade of superstars, including Michael Jackson, Quincy Jones, Diana Ross, Elton John, Rick Astley, and Vanessa Williams. In addition he has launched the careers of dozens of artists, including Tramaine Hawkins and the Winans.

Through the years Andraé Crouch's energies were devoted to performing live, often accompanied by his renowned singers and band members. He has performed in sixty-eight countries and consistently sells out concert halls throughout Europe, America, and the Far East.

In Japan, for example, his debut concert tour created instant pandemonium, a phenomenon repeated in some new Crouch strongholds as South Africa, where a local gospel choir has even named themselves after him. His music has been translated into twenty-one languages, and from Finland to Barbados, Andraé Crouch has proven himself a world-class concert attraction.

Crouch's reputation as a live performer is matched by his standing as a producer, writer, and arranger. In recent years he has served as vocal arranger for Michael Jackson's Grammy-nominated smash hit "Man in the Mirror," which featured the distinctive vocal accompaniment of the Andraé Crouch Singers. In the year 2001, the sound of the Crouch Singers was again heard on Michael Jackson's much anticipated comeback album, *Invincible*.

Andraé Crouch and his singers also worked on tracks for Quincy Jones' groundbreaking 1990 album, *Back on the Block*. Later Crouch and Jones teamed up again on Steven Spielberg's film *The Color Purple*, and Crouch served as gospel historian for the movie as well as arranger of all the soundtrack's choir segments. In addition, he cowrote the rousing "Maybe God Is Trying to Tell You Something."

More of his notable writing, producing, and arranging credits include the score to the animated feature film *Once Upon a Forest* and the animated Disney film *The Lion King*; the Michael Jackson–performed "Will You Be There" from the hit film *Free Willy*; the title theme from the television comedy *Amen;* the Quincy Jones–produced *Handel's_Messiah: A Soulful Celebration*; as well as "The Power," a song on the duet album from Elton John featuring Little Richard. The Turner Broadcasting Television special on Dr. Seuss, featuring the classic *Yertle the Turtle,* not only has music cowritten by Andraé Crouch but also highlighted the artist as Yertle himself. He also wrote an arrangement of "Precious Lord Take My Hand" for the 1996 film adaptation of John Grisham's 1989 legal thriller *A Time to Kill.*

Andraé Crouch was at the pinnacle of an extraordinary career when he was faced with a choice that would change, once and for all, the direction of his life. The death of his mother, followed in quick succession by the passing of his father and brother, placed the future of the Christ Memorial Church, built by the Crouch family over forty years ago, on the shoulders of the younger son, Andraé. The decision to answer the call to ministry was made all the more difficult in the light of the extraordinary professional accomplishments Andraé Crouch had made in recent years. His 1994 Qwest Records release, *Mercy*, had landed the artist his seventh Grammy award, this time for *Best Pop Contemporary Gospel Album*, attesting to his proven ability to reach audiences on both the pop/gospel divide. Andraé Crouch's universal appeal was also the impetus for the Grammy-winning *Tribute: The Songs of Andraé Crouch*, the 1996 album saluting his enduring musical contributions. The collection of songs was performed by artists including The Brooklyn Tabernacle Choir, Take 6, Michael W. Smith, and the Winans. *Tribute* was named *Best Contemporary Gospel Album* at the 1997 Grammy Awards.

On the difficult decision of answering the call to ministry, Crouch reveals, "I thought if I took up the mantle of pastor I wouldn't be able to make music my first priority, and initially I was filled with doubt about making such a choice. But God just pointed out to me that He had given me everything I had and that He wasn't about to take anything away. I slowly came to understand that He was adding to my life and ministry, and that music was as much a part of both as it had ever been." He now shares the pastoral responsibility with his twin sister, Sandra Crouch, who is the co-pastor at the New Christ Memorial Church.

It was in 1996 that Crouch found himself able to commit the time and energy to return to the recording studio and begin work on the album that would become *Pray*. "The title was no accident," he says with a chuckle. "Every step of the way I was depending on the grace of God—and the good will of the musicians—to bring the music to life. It's one thing to sing a song all alone in the morning, but it's a whole other challenge to capture that feeling in a recording studio."

Crouch also recorded *The Gift of Christmas*, a panorama of songs ranging from new renditions of the American Christmas song treasures to beautiful originals like "Bethlehem" and "Take Me to Jesus."

Now, while actively fulfilling the role of pastor, including everything from preaching to counseling to community outreach, Crouch finds himself inspired to write some of the best, most direct and honest, new music. God has taken him a step further when in the spring of 2002 he opened his own record label. After having been a part of some of the largest secular record labels for decades, Crouch has ventured out and has established his own record label, where he has introduced brand-new talents as well as continuing his own recording career. The name of the label is *Slave Records*, referring to Scripture passages that state that we must choose to be slaves (servants) of God.

In 2006 Andraé Crouch released *Mighty Wind*, a fortieth anniversary album featuring guest performances by Marvin Winans, Crystal Lewis, Fred Hammond, Karen Clark Sheard, and Marcus Cole. His latest recording, a single entitled "The Promise," which became available in stores February 15, 2011, continues to showcase his musical talent and versatility.

Andraé Crouch has won numerous awards and honors over the years, including nine Grammy Awards; four Gospel Music Association Doves; and ASCAP, Billboard, and NAACP Awards. On June 4, 2004, he became the only living Gospel artist, and just the third in history, to have a star on the Hollywood Walk of Fame. Still today, fans, fellow musicians, and the Christian community as a whole see him as one of the most renowned and widely respected pioneers of contemporary Gospel music.

Special "Thank You"

I AM SO INDEBTED to the following individuals who partnered with me in bringing this book to publication. Without their financial investment, you would not have been able to hold *The Most Important Word* in your hands right now. My sincerest gratitude and love go out to them, as some took the leap of faith and blessed me out of their "nothings."

Thank you…Clarence and Dr. Caretha Crawford, Jay and Laura Nicholls, Lea J. Philippe, Donna James, Wanda Myers, Minnie Turner, Winston and Juliet Maxwell, Delroy and Patela Oakley, Gregory and Ruth Franks, Jeanie Smiling, Winona W. James, Jennifer Lucas, Esq.

Keith, Michele, and Judah Duncan; Dervent and Audrey Wiltshire; Myron and Sandra Davis; Ruth Burrell; Elaine Hutchinson; Patricia Fingal; and Daniel Pearson and Heather Richardson.

I want to also thank those of you who gave as best you could. Although you could not meet what was necessary to invest, you still wanted to contribute somehow. For this I say, "Thank you." There were so many others who wanted to assist me in this venture but were not financially able. To them I also say, "Thank You," as their hearts were truly willing.

Contact the Author

For more information about Hewlette Pearson and her speaking and book signing events, please visit:

www.hewlettepearson.com

Speaking Engagement:

contact@hewlettepearson.com

E-mail: info@hewlettepearson.com